Contents

 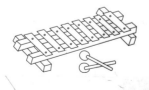

Using This Activity Book

In this little book, you'll find an activity sheet tied to each book in the set (and each letter of the alphabet). Each sheet includes: practice in writing both upper- and lowercase letters, a picture to color, and a chance to read more words that begin with the letter. Here are a few tips on how to get the most out of the activities.

- Let your child complete the activity sheet after you've read the book a few times. This way, he or she will be more familiar with the target letter.

- Help your child read the directions. Then have your child trace each letter with a finger. Point out the arrows and numbers that show how to make the lines and curves. Next, your child can write over the dashed letter with a pencil. Use the rest of the line to let your child write the letter independently.

- Help your child sound out the words in the box, reading them a few times. Then let your child color the picture.

- At the end of the book, you'll find three bonus review activities. Use these after you've read the complete set to show how much your child has learned!

Nonfiction Alphabet Readers © Scholastic

More Fun Alphabet Activities

The more practice your child gets with letters, the closer he or she comes to being a great reader! These quick and easy ideas make learning fun—anytime!

- Letters are all around you, everywhere you go! Choose a letter of the alphabet and go on a "scavenger hunt" as you go through your daily routine. Simply challenge your child to spot the letter on street signs, on food labels at the grocery store, and so on. You might even keep count, for instance: how many *b*'s did you find at the bank? At least one, for sure!

- Eat the alphabet! There are lots of products that feature letters for your child to name. Try bringing home alphabet soup, cooking up some alphabet noodles, or eating alphabet cereal. Pick a letter and see how many your child can find and eat!

- Play a game of "I Spy" in the car or on a walk. Give your child an alphabet clue along with a little hint, such as "I spy something with leaves and branches that starts with the letter *t*." Your child can then point to the tree and say the word aloud—and have a lot of fun learning letters!

A is for apple.

Read these words:

apple

autumn

ape

Trace and write the letters.

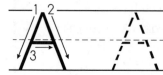

4

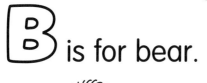 **B** is for bear.

Read these words:

bear
beautiful
baby

Trace and write the letters.

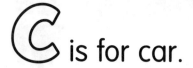 **is for car.**

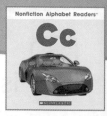

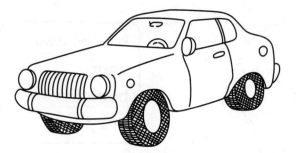

Read these words:

car
colorful
cute

Trace and write the letters.

D is for dog.

Read these words:

dog
dream
dinner

Trace and write the letters.

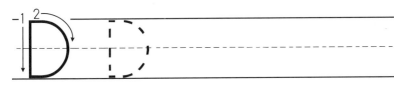

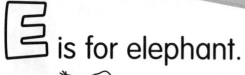 is for elephant.

Read these words:

elephant

earth

eat

Trace and write the letters.

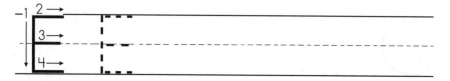

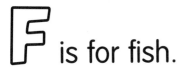 **is for fish.**

Read these words:

fish

fast

football

Trace and write the letters.

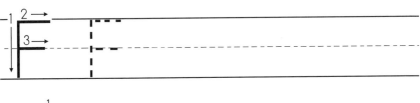

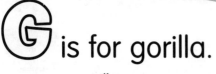 **G** is for gorilla.

Read these words:

gorilla

good

goofy

Trace and write the letters.

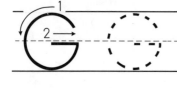

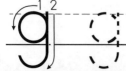

10   Nonfiction Alphabet Readers © Scholastic

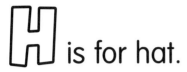 is for hat.

Read these words:

hat

head

hot dog

Trace and write the letters.

I is for ice cream.

Read these words:

ice cream

is

invite

Trace and write the letters.

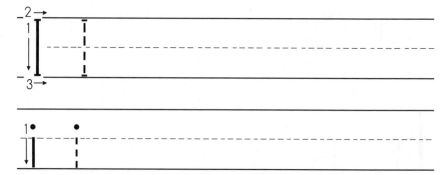

J is for jaguar.

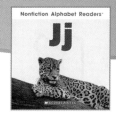

Read these words:

jaguar
jungle
jump

Trace and write the letters.

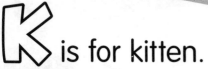 is for kitten.

Read these words:

kitten

key

kiss

Trace and write the letters.

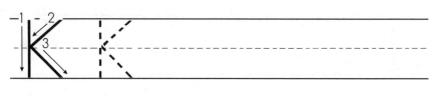

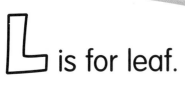 is for leaf.

Read these words:

leaf
large
learn

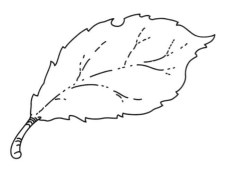

Trace and write the letters.

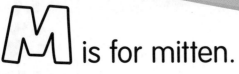 **is for mitten.**

Read these words:

mitten
match
melt

Trace and write the letters.

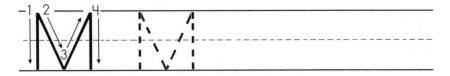

Nonfiction Alphabet Readers © Scholastic

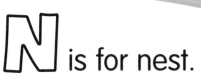 is for nest.

Read these words:

nest
nice
nibble

Trace and write the letters.

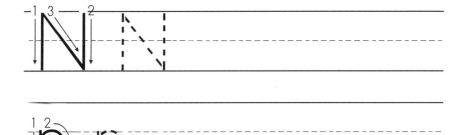

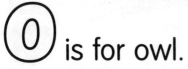 is for owl.

Nonfiction Alphabet Readers

Read these words:

owl

open

orange

Trace and write the letters.

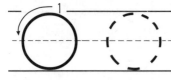

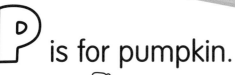 **P** is for pumpkin.

Read these words:

pumpkin
patch
perfect

Trace and write the letters.

Q is for quilt.

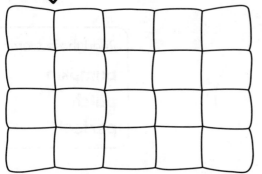

Read these words:

quilt

queen

quick

Trace and write the letters.

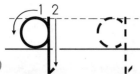

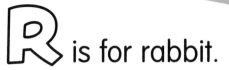 **R** is for rabbit.

Read these words:

rabbit

run

rock

Trace and write the letters.

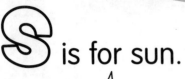 **S** is for sun.

Read these words:

sun

season

sailboat

Trace and write the letters.

Nonfiction Alphabet Readers © Scholastic

T is for turtle.

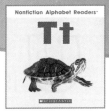

Read these words:

turtle
tiny
take

Trace and write the letters.

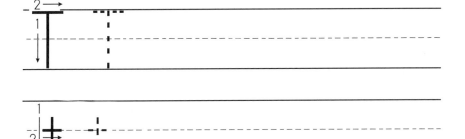

U is for umbrella.

Trace and write the letters.

Nonfiction Alphabet Readers © Scholastic

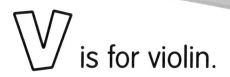 is for violin.

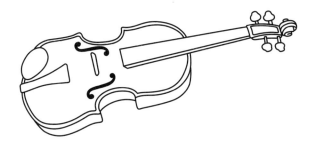

Read these words:

violin

very

vote

Trace and write the letters.

W is for web.

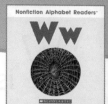

Read these words:

web

weave

work

Trace and write the letters.

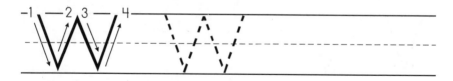

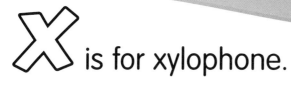 is for xylophone.

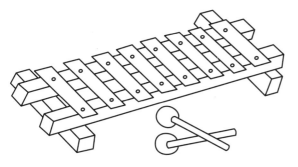

Read these words:

xylophone
excellent
exciting

Trace and write the letters.

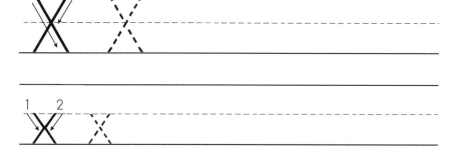

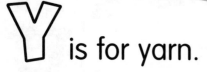 **is for yarn.**

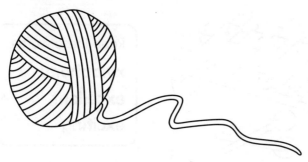

Read these words:

yarn
yak
yellow

Trace and write the letters.

28

Z is for zebra.

Read these words:

zebra

zoo

zoom

Trace and write the letters.

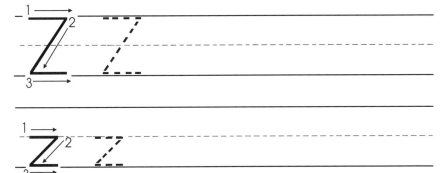

Fill in the missing letters.

A B C ☐ E F ☐

H ☐ J K ☐ M N

☐ P Q R S ☐ U

V ☐ X Y Z

Connect the letters in order to make a picture.

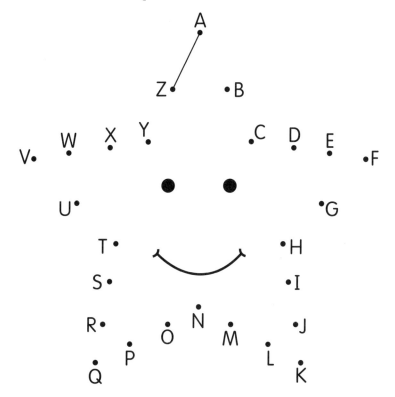

Write your name on the line.

_____

- -

_____

Draw something that begins with the same letter as your name.

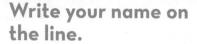

Dear Parents,

Learning the alphabet is an exciting accomplishment for young children, and this handy little box is packed with ways to help your child do just that! Inside, you'll find 26 books—one for each letter of the alphabet. These bright, colorful books are tied to children's favorite nonfiction topics, making them irresistible as well as educational. From A is for apple to Z is for zebra, beautiful photos make every letter come to life. Plus, each book is brimming with words that begin with the target letter, so children get plenty of exposure to each letter's shape and sound. But that's not all—in this set you also get a mini-activity book to give your child even more practice writing and reading each letter, and 16 motivational stickers to reward their learning!

Understanding the relationships between letters and the sounds they make is a key step on the road to reading success. But you don't have to be a literacy expert to help teach your child to read. This little guide is filled with tips to maximize learning opportunities—so while your child is becoming a great reader, you're becoming a great teacher! With the Nonfiction Alphabet Readers set, your child will soon be singing "Now I know my ABC's" with pride!

Enjoy!
The Editors

Tips for Using the
Nonfiction Alphabet Readers Set

To foster a love of reading in your child, try to make it
a special activity that you share and look forward to.
Choose a time of day (such as bedtime, or after dinner)
when both you and your child can slow down, relax, and
"curl up with a good book." You might even choose a
special, cozy spot for reading together. This will not only
show your child that reading is important, but also that it's a way of having family
fun, just like doing a puzzle or playing a board game—or maybe even better!

To help your child learn each letter, we suggest you read every book in the set
several times. Here are some more tips to help you and your child get the most out
of all the goodies in this little box!

Before You Read

- Look at the cover and invite your child to name the letter. You can also
  encourage your child to trace both the uppercase and the lowercase letter with
  his or her finger.

- Next, ask your child what sound the letter makes. Keep in mind than some
  letters make more than one sound. For instance, if you're reading the Aa book
  you might point out, "Sometimes a makes the ah sound, like in *apple*. Other
  times it makes the ay sound, like in *ape*."

- Now point out the photo on the cover and invite your child to tell what it shows. Why might the author have chosen to show that particular thing? Because its name starts with the featured letter! Ask your child to tell what they know about the subject of the book, for example, "Where do apples grow? What do they taste like? What colors do apples come in?"

As You Read

- As you read the book for the first time, let your child look at the photographs and listen to the language. If there are any vocabulary words your child might not know, talk about their meanings. Encourage your child to notice how the photos relate to the words—how do they help show what the words say?

- The next time you read the book, point out the words in bold print. Why did the author make these words stand out? Here's a hint: look at the first letter in each one! Read the words together, and review the sound the letter makes in each word.

- As you do more readings, encourage your child to follow the print with a finger as you read the words aloud, trying to match the printed words with the spoken ones. After a while, your child may be able to join in

A is for **apple**.

Apples grow on **apple** trees.

and read some of the book with you, or even read the whole thing by themselves! It's okay if your child's "reading" is really coming from memorization—just handling books and speaking the words aloud with expression are important steps in early literacy!

After You Read

- Talk together about the book's subject. For instance, ask, "What is one new thing you learned about apples? What do you know about apples that was not in the book?" You can also ask your child to point out his or her favorite photographs.

- Now do the corresponding activity sheet in the mini-activity book. You can do it together, or read the directions and then let your child try to complete it by him or herself. Finally, celebrate your child's accomplishments with the included stickers. You can stick them on an activity sheet to show a job well done, surprise your child by slipping one into a lunch bag, or even stick one on your child's shirt to wear proudly to school!

4

OTH5651131

Nonfiction Alphabet Readers™

by Liza Charlesworth

SCHOLASTIC INC.

NEW YORK • TORONTO • LONDON • AUCKLAND • SYDNEY • MEXICO CITY • NEW DELHI • HONG KONG

Photographs © 2012: Getty Images/Heinrich van den Berg: 7; iStockphoto: 8 (Christine Keene), 3 (Gabor Izso), cover, back cover, 2 (Marek Mnich), 5 (Sharon Meredith), 1, 9 (Valeria Tarleva); Media Bakery/Richard Lewisohn: 6; Shutterstock, Inc./Sofarina79: 4.

ISBN 978-0-545-49506-6

Cover and interior design by Grafica, Inc.

12 11 10 9 8 7 6 5 4 3 2 1   14 15 16 17 18 19/0

Printed in China   145

A is for **apple**.

Apples grow on **apple** trees.

You can pick **apples** in **autumn**.

There **are all** different
kinds of **apples**.

Kids love **apples**.
Adults love **apples**.

Even **apes** love **apples**!

Apples are awesome!

Nonfiction Alphabet Readers™

by Liza Charlesworth

SCHOLASTIC INC.

NEW YORK • TORONTO • LONDON • AUCKLAND • SYDNEY • MEXICO CITY • NEW DELHI • HONG KONG

Photographs © 2012: Getty Images/Joel Sartore: cover, back cover, 2; iStockphoto: 6 right upper middle (Antagain), 6 bottom right (Dave White), 1, 9 (Eric Isselée), 6 right lower middle (Uros Petrovic); Media Bakery/Paul Souders: 8; Superstock, Inc.: 7 (age fotostock), 3 (Minden Pictures), 6 top right (Photocuisine), 6 background (Stock Connection), 5 (Woodfall Wild Images/Photoshoot/NHPA).

ISBN 978-0-545-49505-9

Cover and interior design by Grafica, Inc.

12 11 10 9 8 7 6 5 4 3 2 1   14 15 16 17 18 19/0

Printed in China   145

B is for **bear**.

Bears are **beautiful**!

Most **bears** are **big**.

But some **bears** are little.
This **baby bear** was just
born!

Bear Food

Bears eat fish, **bugs**, **berries**, and honey made **by bees**.

Bears sleep in caves
and **bathe** in rivers.

Bears are the **best**!

Nonfiction Alphabet Readers™

by Liza Charlesworth

SCHOLASTIC INC.

NEW YORK • TORONTO • LONDON • AUCKLAND • SYDNEY • MEXICO CITY • NEW DELHI • HONG KONG

Photographs © 2012: Alamy Images: 5 (JLImages), 6 (John Cairns); Corbis Images/Katy Winn: 7;
iStockphoto: cover, back cover, 2 (pagadesign), 1, 9 (Stan Rohrer), 3 (Tomasz Pietryszek);
Media Bakery/Dmitri Vervitsiotis: 8; Superstock, Inc./Transtock: 4.

ISBN 978-0-545-49504-2

Cover and interior design by Grafica, Inc.

12 11 10 9 8 7 6 5 4 3 2 1   14 15 16 17 18 19/0

Printed in China   145

C is for **car**.

Cars are **cool**!

This is a race **car**.
It **can** go really fast
around a **curve**!

This **car** is **called** a **cab**.
It **can** take you all over
town!

This **car** is **covered**
with **colorful** flowers.

This **car** is **cute**.
It looks like a **cat**!

This toy **car** is for kids.
How **cool**!

Nonfiction Alphabet Readers™

Dd

by Liza Charlesworth

SCHOLASTIC INC.

NEW YORK • TORONTO • LONDON • AUCKLAND • SYDNEY • MEXICO CITY • NEW DELHI • HONG KONG

Photographs © 2012: Getty Images: 8 (Arthur Tilley/Workbook Stock), 3 (Chris Stein/Lifesize), 6 background (Isabelle Schnoeckel); iStockphoto: 7 (AVAVA), 6 inset (DNY59), cover, back cover, 2 (Eric Isselée), 4 (happy border), 1, 9 (Milan Lipowski), 5 (Robert Simon).

ISBN 978-0-545-49503-5

Cover and interior design by Grafica, Inc.

12 11 10 9 8 7 6 5 4 3 2 1   14 15 16 17 18 19/0

Printed in China   145

D is for **dog**.

Dogs can **do dozens** of things.

Dogs can **dash**.

Dogs can **dig**.
Dogs can get **dirty**, too.

Dogs can lie **down** on **decks** and **dream** all **day**.

Dogs can eat **dinner** from **dishes**.

Dogs are never **dull**.
Dogs are **delightful**!

Nonfiction Alphabet Readers™

by Liza Charlesworth

SCHOLASTIC INC.

NEW YORK • TORONTO • LONDON • AUCKLAND • SYDNEY • MEXICO CITY • NEW DELHI • HONG KONG

Photographs © 2012: iStockphoto: 5 (Christophe Cerisier), 8 (Jurie Maree), 7 (Peter Malsbury), cover, back cover, 2 (shipfactory); Media Bakery: 1, 9 (Digital Zoo), 4 (Laurie Excell), 3 (Theo Allofs), 6.

ISBN 978-0-545-49502-8

Cover and interior design by Grafica, Inc.

12 11 10 9 8 7 6 5 4 3 2 1   14 15 16 17 18 19/0

Printed in China   145

E is for **elephant**.

Elephants are **enormous!**

Elephants are the most **enormous** animals that walk on **earth**.

ear

Elephants have **enormous ears**. Their hearing is **excellent**.

trunk

Elephants have **enormous** trunks. They use their trunks to **eat**!

Elephants have **enormous** fun playing with **each** other.

It is **easy** to love **elephants**.
They are **exciting**!

Nonfiction Alphabet Readers™

by Liza Charlesworth

SCHOLASTIC INC.

NEW YORK • TORONTO • LONDON • AUCKLAND • SYDNEY • MEXICO CITY • NEW DELHI • HONG KONG

Photographs © 2012: Getty Images: 8 (Jose Luis Pelaez), 4 (Tobias Bernhard); iStockphoto: 1, 9 (alxpin), 6 inset (Antagain), 7 inset (Anthia Cumming), 3 (cynoclub), 6 (EXTREME-PHOTOGRAPHER), cover, back cover, 2 (Peter Lora); Minden Pictures/Doc White: 7; Superstock, Inc./NHPA: 5.

ISBN 978-0-545-49501-1

Cover and interior design by Grafica, Inc.

12 11 10 9 8 7 6 5 4 3 2 1   14 15 16 17 18 19/0

Printed in China   145

F is for **fish**.

Want to meet some **fantastic fish**?

fins

This **fish** is **fast**.
It uses its **fins** to swim.

This **fish** is **fierce**.
It is called a shark.

This **fish** is **fancy**.
It looks like a **fan**!

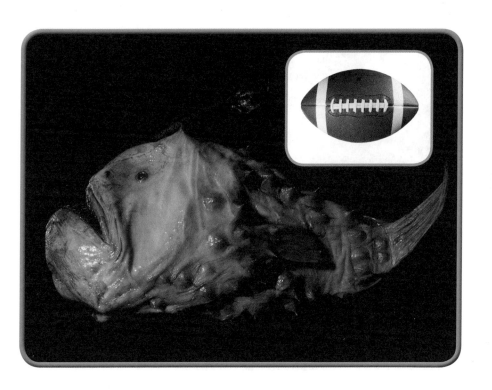

This **fish** is **funny**.
It looks like a **football**!

Fish are **fantastic**.
That is a **fact**!

Nonfiction Alphabet Readers™

Gg

by Liza Charlesworth

SCHOLASTIC INC.

NEW YORK • TORONTO • LONDON • AUCKLAND • SYDNEY • MEXICO CITY • NEW DELHI • HONG KONG

Photographs © 2012: Big Stock Photo/gravesy: 5; Getty Images: 8 (Laurance B. Aiuppy), 4 (Michael Nichols/National Geographic); iStockphoto: 3 (Alan Lagadu), 1, 9 (Eric Isselée); Shutterstock, Inc./fotosav: 5 inset; Superstock, Inc.: 6 (Animals Animals), cover, back cover, 2, 7 (Tier und Naturfotografie).

ISBN 978-0-545-49500-4

Cover and interior design by Grafica, Inc.

12 11 10 9 8 7 6 5 4 3 2 1   14 15 16 17 18 19/0

Printed in China   145

G is for **gorilla**.

Gorillas are **good**
at a lot of things.

Gorillas are **good**
at swinging.
Go, gorilla, go!

Gorillas are **good** at **getting** bananas.

Gorillas are **good** at
giving hugs!

Gorillas are **good** at being **goofy**.

Gorillas are **good** at **going** to sleep.
Good night, big **guy**!

Nonfiction Alphabet Readers™

by Liza Charlesworth

SCHOLASTIC INC.

NEW YORK • TORONTO • LONDON • AUCKLAND • SYDNEY • MEXICO CITY • NEW DELHI • HONG KONG

Photographs © 2012: Getty Images/VisitBritain/Rod Edwards: 4; iStockphoto: 8 (Andrew Rich),
cover, back cover, 2 (Antagain), 5 (David Jones), 7 (Kathryn Carey Spence),
1, 9 (repOrter), 3 (Tabitha Patrick); Media Bakery: 6.

ISBN 978-0-545-49499-1

Cover and interior design by Grafica, Inc.

12 11 10 9 8 7 6 5 4 3 2 1   14 15 16 17 18 19/0
Printed in China   145

H is for **hat**.

My **hat has hearts**.

My **hat has horns**.

My **hat** is **hard**. It **helps** keep my **head** safe.

My **hat** is very **high**.

My **hat** looks like a
hot dog. **How hilarious**!

7

My **hat** makes me **happy**!

8

Nonfiction Alphabet Readers™

by Liza Charlesworth

SCHOLASTIC INC.

NEW YORK • TORONTO • LONDON • AUCKLAND • SYDNEY • MEXICO CITY • NEW DELHI • HONG KONG

Photographs © 2012: Getty Images/Daniel Hurst Photography: 6; iStockphoto: cover, back cover, 2 (DNY59), 1, 9 (Edie Layland), 7 inset (Liudmila Chernova); Media Bakery: 5 (Andersen Ross), 8 (Corbis), 4 (Stuart Gregory), 3; Superstock, Inc./NovaStock: 7.

ISBN 978-0-545-49498-4

Cover and interior design by Grafica, Inc.

12 11 10 9 8 7 6 5 4 3 2 1   14 15 16 17 18 19/0

Printed in China   145

I is for **ice cream**.

I love **ice cream**!
You love **ice cream**!

Even **itty-bitty** kids love **ice cream**!

Ice cream is icy cold
and oh so sweet!

I love to **invite** my friends
over for **ice cream**.

I love to eat **it in**
my **inner tube**.

I can't **imagine** life
without **ice cream**.
It is incredible!

Nonfiction Alphabet Readers™

by Liza Charlesworth

SCHOLASTIC INC.

NEW YORK • TORONTO • LONDON • AUCKLAND • SYDNEY • MEXICO CITY • NEW DELHI • HONG KONG

Photographs © 2012: Getty Images: 5 (Carol FArneti-Foster/Oxford Scientific); 1, 9 (Jerry Young/Dorling Kindersley); cover, back cover, 2 (Steve Kaufman/AWL Images); iStockphoto: 6 inset (GMosher); 3 (Stephen Meese); Media Bakery: 7 (DLILLC), 6 inset (Lu Guangwei); 4 (Tom Brakefield); Shutterstock, Inc./Stephen Meese: 8; Superstock, Inc./Minden Pictures: 6 background.

ISBN 978-0-545-49497-7

Cover and interior design by Grafica, Inc.

12 11 10 9 8 7 6 5 4 3 2 1   14 15 16 17 18 19/0

Printed in China   145

J is for **jaguar**.

Jaguars are **just** amazing!

Jaguars are huge cats.
They live in the **jungle**.

jaws

Jaguars have sharp teeth
and powerful **jaws**.

Jaguars are great
runners. They can go
as fast as a **jeep**!

Jaguars are great **jumpers**, too. **Just** look at that cat go!

Jaguars fill me with **joy**!

Nonfiction Alphabet Readers™

Kk

by Liza Charlesworth

SCHOLASTIC INC.

NEW YORK • TORONTO • LONDON • AUCKLAND • SYDNEY • MEXICO CITY • NEW DELHI • HONG KONG

Photographs © 2012: Getty Images/Arthur Tilley: 3 (Arthur Tilley); iStockphoto: 6 crown (Alexander Shirokov), cover, back cover, 2 (Kadir Barcin), 6 background (Mehmet Salih Guler), 5 inset (nolimitpictures), 7 (Prill Mediendesign & Fotografie), 5 background (Vasiliy Koval); Media Bakery: 4 (David De Lossy), 8 (Judith Haeusler); Shutterstock, Inc./Utekhina Anna: 1, 9.

ISBN 978-0-545-49496-0

Cover and interior design by Grafica, Inc.

12 11 10 9 8 7 6 5 4 3 2 1   14 15 16 17 18 19/0

Printed in China   145

K is for **kitten**.

Why do **kids** love **kittens**?

Kittens can give **kisses**.

Kittens can play with **keys**.

Kittens can look like **kings**.

Kittens can get into
all **kinds** of trouble!

Kittens can **keep kids** company.

Nonfiction Alphabet Readers™

by Liza Charlesworth

SCHOLASTIC INC.

NEW YORK • TORONTO • LONDON • AUCKLAND • SYDNEY • MEXICO CITY • NEW DELHI • HONG KONG

Photographs © 2012: Getty Images/Michael Melford/The Image Bank: 4, 5; iStockphoto: cover, back cover, 2 (Gansovsky Vladislav), 8 (Gregory Vasil), 3 (Linda Kloosterhof), 1, 9 (mattjeacock); Media Bakery: 7 (Don Farrall), 6 (PHOTO 24).

ISBN 978-0-545-49495-3
Cover and interior design by Grafica, Inc.

12 11 10 9 8 7 6 5 4 3 2 1   14 15 16 17 18 19/0
Printed in China   145

L is for **leaf**.

Do you **like leaves**?
Let's learn all about
them!

Leaves are green
in summer.

But **leaves** change color in **late** fall.

The **leaves** turn yellow,
red, and orange.
How **lovely**!

Then, the **leaves let** go
of the tree **limbs** and
fall to the ground.

Look at that **large** pile
of **leaves**. **Let's leap**!

Nonfiction Alphabet Readers™

by Liza Charlesworth

SCHOLASTIC INC.

NEW YORK • TORONTO • LONDON • AUCKLAND • SYDNEY • MEXICO CITY • NEW DELHI • HONG KONG

Photographs © 2012: Getty Images/Ariel Skelley: 6; iStockphoto: 5 (Alexey Astakhov), cover, back cover, 2 (Liudmila Evdochimova), 1, 9 (Sally Scott); Media Bakery: 8 (Brigitte Sporrer), 3, 4; Shutterstock, Inc./Renata Osinska: 7.

ISBN 978-0-545-49494-6

Cover and interior design by Grafica, Inc.

12 11 10 9 8 7 6 5 4 3 2 1   14 15 16 17 18 19/0

Printed in China   145

M is for **mittens**.

Mittens make me happy. They keep **my** hands warm.

Mittens match.
Each has a **mate**.

Mittens come in **many** colors and patterns.

Mittens are great for **making** snowmen.

Mittens are great for
holding **melty** icicles, too.

I'll **miss my mittens**
when winter is over!

Nonfiction Alphabet Readers™

by Liza Charlesworth

SCHOLASTIC INC.

NEW YORK • TORONTO • LONDON • AUCKLAND • SYDNEY • MEXICO CITY • NEW DELHI • HONG KONG

Photographs © 2012: Getty Images: 5 (Laura Zenker/SinglEye Photography), 6 (Leah Fauller); iStockphoto: 8 (Don Nichols), 7 (James Brey), 1, 9 (Mayr Budny), Media Bakery/Siede Preis: cover, back cover, 2; Superstock, Inc.: 4 (age fotostock), 3 (Animals Animals).

ISBN 978-0-545-49493-9

Cover and interior design by Grafica, Inc.

12 11 10 9 8 7 6 5 4 3 2 1   14 15 16 17 18 19/0

Printed in China   145

N is for **nest**.

What do you **notice**
up in the tree?
A **nice nest**!

What do you **notice**
inside the **nest**?
Nice eggs!

What is hatching from
the **nice** eggs?
New babies!

The **new** babies are
noisy. They are also
hungry.

So mother bird brings
the **new** babies a
worm to **nibble**.

It is **now** time for a
nap. **Nighty-night,
new** babies!

Nonfiction Alphabet Readers™

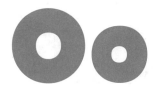

by Liza Charlesworth

SCHOLASTIC INC.

NEW YORK • TORONTO • LONDON • AUCKLAND • SYDNEY • MEXICO CITY • NEW DELHI • HONG KONG

Photographs © 2012: Getty Images/Art Wolfe: 3; iStockphoto: 4 (Agnieszka Szymczak), cover, back cover, 1, 2, 9 (Eric Isselée);
Superstock, Inc.: 6 (age fotostock), 5 (Alessandro Canova/Marka), 8 (National Geographic),
7 (Wayne Lynch/All Canada Photos).

ISBN 978-0-545-49492-2

Cover and interior design by Grafica, Inc.

12 11 10 9 8 7 6 5 4 3 2 1   14 15 16 17 18 19/0

Printed in China   145

O is for **owl**.

Oh! I see an **owl**
peeking **out of** a hole.

Oh! I see an **owl** sitting **on** the branch **of** an **old oak** tree.

Oh! I see an **owl** with bright **orange** eyes. How **odd**!

Oh! I see an **owl opening** up its wings.

Oh! I see an **owl** flying **out over** a snowy field.

Oh! I do love **owls**!

Nonfiction Alphabet Readers™

Pp

by Liza Charlesworth

SCHOLASTIC INC.

NEW YORK • TORONTO • LONDON • AUCKLAND • SYDNEY • MEXICO CITY • NEW DELHI • HONG KONG

Photographs © 2012: Dreamstime/Kenneth Graff: 4; iStockphoto: 1, 9 (Creativeye99), 3 (Isaac Koval), cover (Skip ODonnell), back cover, 2 (Skip ODonnell), Media Bakery: 6 (Dann Tardif/LWA), 5 (KidStock), 7, 8.

ISBN 978-0-545-49490-8

Cover and interior design by Grafica, Inc.

12 11 10 9 8 7 6 5 4 3 2 1   14 15 16 17 18 19/0

Printed in China   145

P is for **pumpkin**.

You can go to a **patch** and **pick pumpkins**.

You can use **pumpkins**
to make a yummy **pie**.

You can **paint pumpkins**.

You can **pull** out the **pulp** and carve **pumpkins**.

You can **put pumpkins** on your **porch**.

Pumpkins are **perfect**!

Nonfiction Alphabet Readers™

by Liza Charlesworth

SCHOLASTIC INC.

NEW YORK • TORONTO • LONDON • AUCKLAND • SYDNEY • MEXICO CITY • NEW DELHI • HONG KONG

Photographs © 2012: Getty Images: 4 (Jeff Smith), 5 background (Mark Polott/Photolibrary), 8 (Matt Carey); iStockphoto/Jessica Key: 7; Media Bakery: 1 (Daniel Hurst), 9 (Daniel Hurst), 5 inset (Matthieu Spohn), 3; Superstock, Inc.: cover, back cover, 2 (Christie's Images), 6 (Exactostock).

ISBN 978-0-545-49489-2

Cover and interior design by Grafica, Inc.

12 11 10 9 8 7 6 5 4 3 2 1   14 15 16 17 18 19/0

Printed in China   145

Q is for **quilt**.

Quick! Let's learn about **quilts**.

Quilts are sewn by hand. They take **quite** a long time to make.

Quilts are **quite** colorful. This one is fit for a **queen**!

Quilts are **quite**
comfortable.

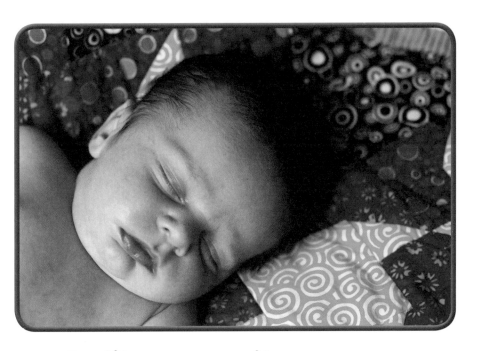

Quilts are **quite** cozy.
Quiet, the baby is
sleeping!

Quilts are **quite** incredible! You can **quote** me on that.

Nonfiction Alphabet Readers™

by Liza Charlesworth

SCHOLASTIC INC.

NEW YORK • TORONTO • LONDON • AUCKLAND • SYDNEY • MEXICO CITY • NEW DELHI • HONG KONG

Photographs © 2012: Dreamstime/Ragnarock: 7 right; Getty Images: 5 (Martin Ruegner/StockImage), 4 (Rolf Kopfle/Peter Arnold); iStockphoto: 7 bottom left (Creativeye99), 6 (Mariya Bibkova); Media Bakery: 1, 9 (GK Hart/Vikki Hart), 3; Shutterstock, Inc.: 7 top left (Anna Kucherova), cover, back cover, 2 (Eric Isselée); Shutterstock, Inc./Julija Sapic: 8.

ISBN 978-0-545-49488-5

Cover and interior design by Grafica, Inc.

Copyright © 2012 by Lefty's Editorial Services. All rights reserved. Published by Scholastic Inc. SCHOLASTIC, NONFICTION ALPHABET READERS, and associated logos are trademarks and/or registered trademarks of Scholastic Inc.

12 11 10 9 8 7 6 5 4 3 2 1   14 15 16 17 18 19/0

Printed in China   145

R is for **rabbit**.

ears ⟶

⟵ tail

Rabbits have long ears
and **round** tails.

Rabbits really like to **run**.

Rabbits really like to **rest**.

Rabbits really like to eat **roots** and vegetables.

carrots

radishes

lettuce

Rabbits really love
carrots, lettuce, and
bright **red radishes**.

Rabbits really rock!

Nonfiction Alphabet Readers™

by Liza Charlesworth

SCHOLASTIC INC.

NEW YORK • TORONTO • LONDON • AUCKLAND • SYDNEY • MEXICO CITY • NEW DELHI • HONG KONG

Photographs © 2012: Getty Images: 3 (Dennis Hallinan), 6 (Harvey Schwartz/Photolibrary), 7 (Image by J. Parsons), 5 (Mike Timo/The Image Bank), 4 (Ron Dahlquist); Media Bakery: cover, back cover, 1, 2, 9 (Ian McKinnell), 8.

ISBN 978-0-545-49487-8

Cover and interior design by Grafica, Inc.

12 11 10 9 8 7 6 5 4 3 2 1   14 15 16 17 18 19/0

Printed in China   145

S is for **sun**.

See the **sun**?
It is a **star**.

The **sun** is **super** big
and **sizzling** hot!

The **sun shines**
in every **season**.

The **sun shines**
on land and **sea**.
See the **sailboat**!

The **sun shines**
on the **sidewalk**.
See the **shadows**!

I like to **sit** in the **sun**.
It is **sensational**!

Nonfiction Alphabet Readers™

by Liza Charlesworth

SCHOLASTIC INC.

NEW YORK • TORONTO • LONDON • AUCKLAND • SYDNEY • MEXICO CITY • NEW DELHI • HONG KONG

Photographs © 2012: Dreamstime/Anna Utekhina: 7 center; iStockphoto: 1, 9 (forcontrast), 7 bottom right (Ivan Kmit), 8 (Jamie Farrant), 7 top right (Magdalena Yaramova); Media Bakery: 6 (altrendo nature), 4 (Bartee Photography), 5 (Joel Sartore), 3 (Jose Luis Pelaez); Shutterstock, Inc.: cover, back cover, 2, 7 top left (anneka), 7 bottom left (fivespots).

ISBN 978-0-545-49486-1

Cover and interior design by Grafica, Inc.

Copyright © 2012 by Lefty's Editorial Services. All rights reserved. Published by Scholastic Inc. SCHOLASTIC, NONFICTION ALPHABET READERS, and associated logos are trademarks and/or registered trademarks of Scholastic Inc.

12 11 10 9 8 7 6 5 4 3 2 1   14 15 16 17 18 19/0

Printed in China   145

T is for **turtle**.

Time to learn about **turtles**!

shell

Turtles have a **tough** shell on **top**.

(4)

beak

Turtles have a beak,
but no **teeth**.

Turtles hatch from
eggs. Baby **turtles**
are so **tiny**!

Do you want **to** see some different **types** of **turtles**? **Take** a look!

Turtles are **terrific**!

Nonfiction Alphabet Readers™

by Liza Charlesworth

SCHOLASTIC INC.

NEW YORK • TORONTO • LONDON • AUCKLAND • SYDNEY • MEXICO CITY • NEW DELHI • HONG KONG

Photographs © 2012: Getty Images: 5 left (Ableimages), 6 right (Andreas Brandt/Digital Vision), 5 right (Dimitri Vervitsiotis), 4 (John and Lisa Merrill/The Image Bank), 8 (Steve Satushek/Workbook Stock); iStockphoto: 1, 9 (Jenny Home), 3 (Judy Barranco), cover, back cover, 2 (Oleksiy Mark); Media Bakery: 6 left (Steve Wisbauer), 7.

ISBN 978-0-545-49485-4

Cover and interior design by Grafica, Inc.

12 11 10 9 8 7 6 5 4 3 2 1   14 15 16 17 18 19/0

Printed in China   145

U is for **umbrella**.

Uh-oh!
It is raining.

Up go the **umbrellas**!

Umbrellas can be big.
Umbrellas can be small.

Umbrellas can be plain.
Umbrellas can be **unusual**!

I love to be **under** my
umbrella...

…**until** the rain stops.

Nonfiction Alphabet Readers™

by Liza Charlesworth

SCHOLASTIC INC.

NEW YORK • TORONTO • LONDON • AUCKLAND • SYDNEY • MEXICO CITY • NEW DELHI • HONG KONG

Photographs © 2012: Getty Images/Ozgur Donmaz: 6; iStockphoto: 1,9 (-art-siberia-), cover, back cover, 2 (Petre Milevski); Media Bakery: 7 (Jose Luis Pelaez), 3, 8 (Mike Kemp), 4; Superstock, Inc./Peter Willi: 5.

ISBN 978-0-545-49484-7

Cover and interior design by Grafica, Inc.

12 11 10 9 8 7 6 5 4 3 2 1   14 15 16 17 18 19/0
Printed in China   145

V is for **violin**.

My name is **Vicki**.
I play the **violin**.

Violins make **very** beautiful music.

Violins have been around for a **very** long time.

Very old people play **violins**.

Very young people play **violins**.

What is the **very** best
instrument on earth?
I **vote** for the **violin**!

Nonfiction Alphabet Readers™

by Liza Charlesworth

SCHOLASTIC INC.

NEW YORK • TORONTO • LONDON • AUCKLAND • SYDNEY • MEXICO CITY • NEW DELHI • HONG KONG

Photographs © 2012: Media Bakery: 8 (ERproductions Ltd), 7 (Frank Krahmer), 4, 5 (Reinhard Holz); Shutterstock, Inc./Pavelk: 6; Superstock, Inc.: 1, 9 (age fotostock), cover, back cover, 2 (Belinda Images), 3 (Minden Pictures).

ISBN 978-0-545-49483-0

Cover and interior design by Grafica, Inc.

12 11 10 9 8 7 6 5 4 3 2 1   14 15 16 17 18 19/0

Printed in China   145

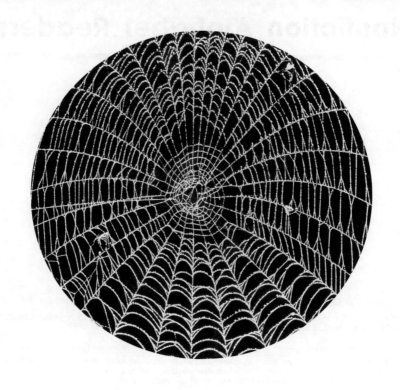

W is for **web**.

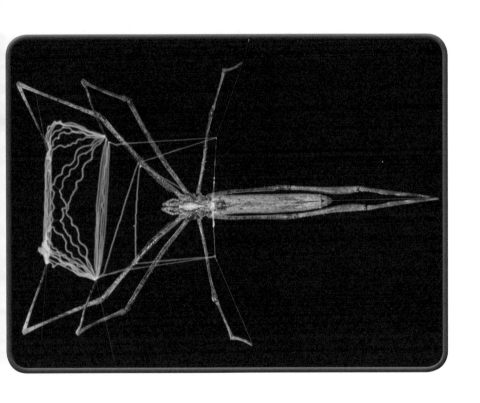

Spiders **weave webs**.

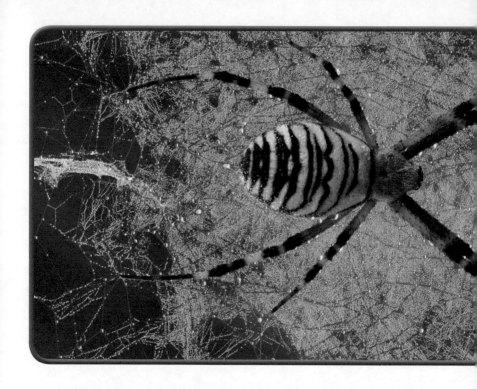

Just **watch** the **way** this spider **works**.

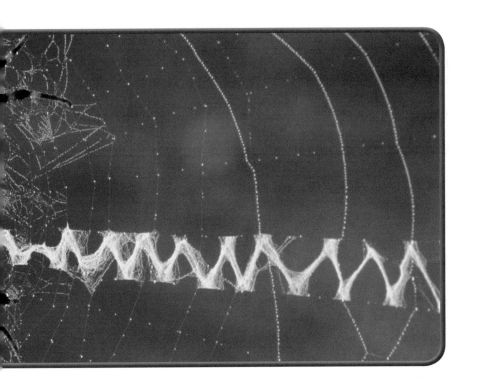

Wow! What a
wonderful web!

No two **webs** are alike.
This **web** is **wet**.

This **web** is shining
in the **warm** sun.

Wow! I **wish** I could
weave a **web**.

Nonfiction Alphabet Readers™

by Liza Charlesworth

SCHOLASTIC INC.

NEW YORK • TORONTO • LONDON • AUCKLAND • SYDNEY • MEXICO CITY • NEW DELHI • HONG KONG

Photographs © 2012: Alamy Images/Inspirestock Inc.: 3; Corbis Images/Lindsay Hebberd: 6, 7; Getty Images: cover, back cover, 2 (Creative Crop/Digital Vision), 5 (IMAGEMORE Co., LTD.), 8 (Shawn James Seymour); iStockphoto/MoniqueRodriguez: 4; Media Bakery/Jules Frazier: 1, 9.

ISBN 978-0-545-49482-3
Cover and interior design by Grafica, Inc.
Copyright © 2012 by Lefty's Editorial Services. All rights reserved. Published by Scholastic Inc. SCHOLASTIC, NONFICTION ALPHABET READERS, and associated logos are trademarks and/or registered trademarks of Scholastic Inc.
12 11 10 9 8 7 6 5 4 3 2 1   14 15 16 17 18 19/0
Printed in China   145

X is for **xylophone**.

A **xylophone** is an **excellent** musical instrument.

A **xylophone** makes **excellent** sounds.

Grownups play
xylophones. Kids play
xylophones, too.

Look at that **extra-long xylophone**!

Wow! It is so
exciting!

XOXOXOXOXOXOXOX!
That means: I love you,
xylophone!

Nonfiction Alphabet Readers™

by Liza Charlesworth

SCHOLASTIC INC.

NEW YORK • TORONTO • LONDON • AUCKLAND • SYDNEY • MEXICO CITY • NEW DELHI • HONG KONG

Photographs © 2012: Getty Images/Andy Crawford/Dorling Kindersley: 8; iStockphoto/Ebru Baraz: 3; Media Bakery: 6; Shutterstock, Inc.: 7 (BlueOrange Studio), cover, back cover, 2 (Dennis and Yulia Pogostins), 4 left, 4 right (Eric Isselée), 5 (shooarts), 1, 9 (Steve Mann).

ISBN 978-0-545-49481-6

Cover and interior design by Grafica, Inc.

12 11 10 9 8 7 6 5 4 3 2 1   14 15 16 17 18 19/0

Printed in China   145

Y is for **yarn**.

Yippee for **yarn**!

Sheep

Yak

Yarn comes from sheep.
Yarn also comes from **yaks**.

You can dye **yarn**
to be red, **yellow**,
green, or blue.

You can use **yarn**
to make a hat. **Yay!**

You can use **yarn**
to make a blanket, too.

Do **you** love **yarn**?
Yell "Yes-siree!"

Nonfiction Alphabet Readers™

by Liza Charlesworth

SCHOLASTIC INC.

NEW YORK • TORONTO • LONDON • AUCKLAND • SYDNEY • MEXICO CITY • NEW DELHI • HONG KONG

Photographs © 2012: Dreamstime/Prapass Wannapinji: cover, back cover, 2; Getty Images: 7 (Berndt Fischer), 8 (Grant Faint); iStockphoto: 4 (Alexandra Draghici), 3 (Brandon Laufenberg), 5 (Johan Swanepoel); Media Bakery/DLILLC: 6 top left; Shutterstock, Inc./Eric Isselée: 1, 9; Superstock, Inc.: 6 right (James Urbach), 6 bottom left (Wayne Lynch/All Canada Photos).

ISBN 978-0-545-49479-3

Cover and interior design by Grafica, Inc.

12 11 10 9 8 7 6 5 4 3 2 1   14 15 16 17 18 19/0

Printed in China   145

Z is for **zebra**.

This is the **zoo**.

This is a **zebra** that
lives in the **zoo**.
His name is **Zack**.

Zack loves to **zoom**
all around the **zoo**.

He **zigs** and **zags** and **zips**!

But all that **zooming zonks** a **zebra** out.

Good night, **Zack**!